The Art of Deathmatch

The Art of Deathmatch

AGLUPPOS

ISBN: 978-952-67944-8-8 (paperback)
ISBN: xxx-xxx-xxxxx-x-x (ePub)

The Wheel Hill

I

I realized I was too drunk to hit
anything with the typewriter so I took a computer
and succeeded to mistype 2 billion times faster

    I was walking with her
    towards the thicket
    when we found a huge sky, got the flies
    our buttocks glittering between the nettles!
    O, we strange!
    I found my way to her valley
    broke into his earthworks
    as the cruel god rapes the earth
    I broke into her like a spear
    makes its way into a monkey
    and the flies loved us

now I am patching it up
poems do not help their writer, and they do not usually teach
no one wants to read them either:

    I don't ask why you left
    I don't search for you
    from the horizon of destruction's lights -
    when you cannot reach to break my specs
    I am not grunting in the night, all alone
    when the one which woke in me, is not carrying me,

like it does
when I'm alone
when my long johns are dirty and I come
naked to your door
when the rays of Sirius are too sharp to be drawn
when you are under my window
and I search, to avoid drowning for you
or anything -

the author prefers not to touch
people walk away, they are like the night
the sun smokes away

telephone rings
Tepe has again messed up his remote control
Antti calls to the regular
car break pad repairs.

II

We call this The Wheel Hill

here days are hung to street lights
hit to the street and kicked
hanged promptly to the branches, shot,
confined in small flats to suffer and suffocate,
drowned in ethanol and methanol and tar

this day
crawled from under the rock right at dawn
like others, I clinked it
to its forehead with my plastic, beery bag

Julle beat up Veka
Ari was jailed, I remember when he chatted
in the bronanza about the fun of stabbing a man
        hey look, dude can't see any more
Rokki steals bikes from the Cultural Centre's yard
    there is always a fight
    whenever I go for a tankard there

Antti was loaded and drove a car to a post,
wrecked it
the cursed road has a full 20 degree turn.

III

Jouko boy sits in the kitchen
Jouko boy sits in the kitchen wearing a shirt
he feels so good
as he has seen
dreams
Jouko boy sits crouched and drinks coffee
at night he drank wine
Jouko boy dreamt that he wept
in the dream he was in a police bus
in police custody on his way to a police jail
the men in the police bus were just like Jouko boy,
hair all over their faces and lost
Jouko boy was reading an AA pamphlet printed upside down
there was a lot of space in the toilet in the police bus
broken door latch
and two children laughing
Jouko boy went
to the can to sit
in that funny way as he sits,
was able to lock the door and woke up
now Jouko boy sits
in the kitchen
drinks coffee and writes.

IV

Angels did not take my poem.
I am afraid of darkness' handiwork in my flat
O God of the Kabbalists
deliver me from trouble

Here I live, in this sort of residence
got walls here and the roof, and lots of dishes
it is as habitual here
as it is not there, of course
you indeed are gods and angels -

I have a cat
he brought a mouse to me, was proud of it
he is probably a perfect being
more perfect than I or my co-men
but he is an animal so we don't give a shit

This is a real good and interesting life, thank you very much.
How you doin' up there?
Lots of evil's excrement to be cleaned?
Tell me, can you spare me a fiver?

V

As I was walking once with Caius
on the wastelands of life

I saw a sphinx who uttered to me thus: if
you know why here in God's arse eye
you trudge with that donkey, tell me:
what goes on four legs in the morning,
at mid-day on two, and in the evening on three?

Speedy Caius quickly in the food store escaped, but me
as laggard felt in my throat, the squeeze of a stony hand

I had heard the riddle earlier and therefore, I answered:
why, you are stone, died in your birth and deserted
the soldiers broke your nose, we are not the same
and you are watching me?

The sphinx sneered, more icily
than any woman ever in my life:
I never got an opportunity, to choose my role or my task,
so why are you evading the answer
when you still have to give it, you blabbering human?

I began to shiver.
Was it that old voice, the ancient mien or what
that hit me like the voice of a broken harp
I fell down like a corpse

and bowed deep in my spirit to that sempiternal:
uh, really sorry, I apologize, I have tried, for real
my best and one cannot ask more from anyone, right?

My horrible teaser's voice deepened when she answered:
Guenon! And that defames the beautiful primates.
Pig! And that as well. Well then, you butt-eye,
you runt aspirant of vanities!

We were here when you still sucked your thumb, pondering
if you preferred Nintendo or jigsaw puzzle for Christmas,
we were here already when you had learned
not to care any more, you self-exalted prick!

You imagine that I would know
mercy or, if it sounds more familiar: sympathy?
Ridiculous! You think it is even allowed?
The gods, and beyond them the fate itself
set me here, by your eroded kiosk path!

My fear grew even worse:
poor me, I was just fetching juice
after a long night, so in most honourable intentions:
oh, if only I had never left at all!

Now this stony monster
after waiting in that familiar willow bush
all her age, perhaps since the beginning of time, who knows,
calls me for reckoning
me, the venerable me who has been so ... inventive

in dire straits, me, who has been so erm
human as only a human can be,
who has resorted to naughtinesses only if no one noticed, yes,
and this is now questioning me??

But I could not escape.

I WAS STONE ALREADY BEFORE YOU WERE BORN,
she thundered,
I already *was* before you were born,
your cheap monkeying
deceives only you yourself, don't you see?
You deaf! You blind! You fool!
And yet, you must answer the question!

I tried to start my cheap moped, cleverly, like I always do
in troubles, not to Sirius, oh no, but all the way to Andromeda
but so futile were my writhings,
the monster grabbed me by the neck, how can it possibly
move so agilely, for such an immobile, immovable one?!
and bullied me even more fiercely:

now you already showed your character, beast!
Were you drinking with Caius again,
seeing you cannot bear a little stare without shaking?
As an orphan leaf in the growl of gale, that's your looks!
But quite green you are still, not snapped loose
in due course, according to the laws!
But as you attempt to dodge my question,
I will present another one to you:

Why do you avoid people, nincompoop?
Why are you wandering here alone? Answer!

Not alone, I stammered, I do got pals too -, I began
but the sphinx interrupted:
stop! There was a tad of truth to that,
which you immediately started to drag back into your mud!
So you recognize your companion? You know
where you belong? To which group?
So you know, after all, who you are?

Not so fast, I groaned, hanging there
at the height of a two ell over the slushy dirt
in a thoroughly uncomfortable position, let me think -
I said, trying to win some time
as not a single fresh word now trickled from my lips.

But I had to answer:
that same stony question had rumbled
on these muddy streets since the beginning of time
and what is even three thousand years to the sphinx?
An instant, a flash of light in a dew drop, not a single breath,
just the space between a question and its answer's echo

and so I would hang here, pierced by the nail
until my mouth dries, until my stomach caterwauls,
in the dash of a wind and rain, until my rags rot,
and that tireless one would still not release me
if nothing came out of my mouth.

All right, okay, I'm a human being. Human, that is
the answer! Has nobody said it to you yet?

Argh I added, just like a comic book hero at his best,
as the sphinx tightened her grip and responded:
a turd you are! A fungus developed a pair of feet,
an aphid shambling without a goal! Where your travelling
finally ends, there will the roses grow rank!
There's your worth, earthling! I have never seen such
a progress, with sails slumped and pissed
without bearing, reason, and purpose!

Now go, she said
and dropped me to the ground on my buttocks,
go, go on your tumbling! Futile is the arm-twisting.
Go your own way and me mine!

I crept quietly away.

Was it really this why the great ones formerly died, I still heard
it muttering in its bushes, while I tried to remember
how to put one in front of the other, thinking
of all these arduous days, dawns white, juiceless.

MY HIGH QUALITY REASON

I am drunk
not enough to get rid of my high-quality reason
but enough to escape this computerized everyday
and this miserable, morning-tinted, grey update

I don't deserve this, in my opinion,
because I am a human being
but because of my aimless acts
I almost apologise to all my loved ones
my father
built the damn country almost by himself

I inherited it all
and I dropped it, now where did it roll, into the sewer?
To rear of the drainboard among butts and potato peels?

When I was toiling, they asked me
what I was doing
and right then
it ceased to interest me, dunno,
just forgot it
all.

MY NONEXISTENT AFFAIRS ARE MINE

My nonexistent affairs are mine
but I am still questioned over them

    right, we hear you (not)
    go on

They sit in a box, in the back of my head and babble
the proofreaders, doctors,
my father of course, and workers and
absolutely everyone

So I begin wondering why
this, and why
thus, and maybe I need to change

No. No bonds!
I am free (and I am afraid)
everything is possible! anything!
as long as nothing has been chosen.

But if I dared to choose and start, I would bitterly regret it
hardly right away but after ten years or maybe twenty
when I'll notice, way too late, that (your habitual here).

THE WORM-EATEN SHIP

Ship, worm-eaten, gnawed by termites
when you finally worked the bottom watertight,
the sails tear and a storm arrives

take interest in anything, be it painting, you will notice
there's not a drop of cinnabar left, or no turpentine
impossible to find suitable cloth, or the very least your cat
pees to your brush just when you found all your gear.

Car, telephone, or computer? Parts disappear, burn through
get bruised faster than you can change them
the one coat is tattered, somebody stole the bike
and turned the hoops to a pile of kinks

there's food, and then there is not
when there is coffee, there are no papers
if you have filter papers, then certainly not milk
if you got milk,
then you will drop the cigarette papers in the kitchen sink

the telly turns on by pulling from the cord
there's no repairing it without a soldering iron
which, unsurprisingly, you cannot afford.

IF A BULLET

If a bullet of iron and lead were to pierce my mind
or steel or uranium, as a paper is pierced
I could not feel my toes any more
nor my feet or my arms,
my silly, dear nose

not the throbbing of my heart, its voice, I would not
know your face any more
and these my memories of you, gone

a red thunder, silent
as I imagine
and no more recollection

just
bloody dust floating
in lazy gravity
and only you are left
to carry what's left of me

How can it happen so fast?
How can anything be so quick?

THE BOTTOM OF THE PIT

Here I lie at the bottom of the pit, tube fed
every day they toss me 10 coppers,
which I reach up to give to the grinning shopkeeper,

every month I get the regular squirrel pelts
half the month I drink, rest I lie sick and eat macaroni

I lie at the bottom of the pit
is it the bad nutrition that damages my brain?
No, I have no strength to climb
but I do hear the steps - I am not deaf

I know there is life out there:
spittle and snot rain down so there are people

a letter
was dropped into the pit: we have work for you
but my watch was measuring moon time
so I missed the talk with the sergeant
at the unemployment office
and they cut my pipe

here I lie again in the pit
I eat macaroni, less ketchup now

no soybeans either

I LISTEN TO THE STEPS

I listen to the steps which pass by, every single one
in Iraq's war 6,000 innocents died
just because the precision weapons always hit
precisely where they chanced to hit

I don't care
as
I am so hardened

after Palestine
after Ireland, Iraq, Somalia
after Afghanistan
Russia and United States and Europe
after the "low intensity conflict"
in the beyond of the moon

meaning: if I left into the space
to the nebula, to the void, to the longing (the beauty!)
and the depths holding galaxies watched me
and maybe my acts
I'm sure I would take along something

to be tooled up, in my hand,
some animal's shank, a pipe, a rusty revolver,
anything with which
I could get blood out
of my comrade I am sharing the cell with

but I was never asked about my politics
I was never asked

as I believed in reincarnation I became aware
as a grey of the north
a staring, unnerving wall doodler
stupid but harmless

is the estimate
for now.

I AM THE WHIP OF GOD

I am the whip of God!
I walk a bone in my hand!

My friend, are you faithful to me?
Now we will go shopping, let me choose
and the purchases we will pay for with a shotgun

every car needs thermite to its roof
ever parking square needs its own thorn carpet
every house an infra-red mine at its doorstep
every town hall a nuclear explosive in its cellar

Nuclear explosive
device often talked about but so misunderstood
a nuclear explosive removes everything visible, up to ten miles
from this place right here where you are reading this

I will ignore the chemical wonder devices, which kill life
more I like to talk
about future's genetic poisons, which according to will
can destroy whole species into extinction
like human beings, all the bunnies, or the starlings

The explosive fuse is also really snug
you can wire it as long straight lines into the ditches
where your enemies take cover
while you shoot them with uranium bullets
then you light the wire and laugh like hell in your hole

Overall, I find absolutely everything awesome
they used to shoot a hundred thousand arrows
        against your attack on a mount
that was apt to sooth and cool blood
the sword may be old-fashioned but just try
today still to talk against a man
who has 600 mm of carefully sharpened steel in his hand

the computer controlled towers of tanks
explosive reactive armor
infrared homing missiles
the aircraft carriers and their fighter legions

man is far too inventive
to survive peace long, but
as interesting times as these
even the Chinese of great Dynasties hardly lived
(in their rare breaks from war and scorn).

THE LAST HOT DAYS

The last hot days of the summer, I put on shorts
and cycle to the town to fetch some cheap rizlas
with such a purposeful and angry attitude
like I had just killed someone 80 times

(as indeed happened but it was a game)

I return all sweaty,
cursing the minuscule clothing of the feminines
satisfied, however, of my defiant reservedness
often, though, forced against a look or a smile,
or laughter, which I didn't want to think about,
or what it could mean.

I am like a tyre
filled to the max, still flat
can't really drive with it
but can't get it any fuller either.

THE PROGRAM ARRANGES

The program arranges the disk.
It is soothing, like washing dishes, I watch
as the entities that have fallen into wrong places are wiped
with moist cloth and things find their proper localities.

I was under attack by the worms and wandering fat
and now this
underprivileged me is allowed to see shining steel!

Consider India: on the street, by the cow shit and fly swarms
drawn by the oxcarts, you can see a shop, selling
broadband connection to the metropolises of our planet.
Or the rows of machines in bank halls:
facing them, who could believe
the leprous are still rolling outside
in their hill cars, begging for their paisas?

Likewise, I forget to think
what's accompanying me now in the soles of my socks
or the slowly leaking valve
of the front tyre of my bicycle.

At the bottom of my refrigerator
there are no onion skins
or juice spots feeding mold
the water falling
behind the window is not wet.

TRADITIONALLY

Traditionally in the television
there has always been a cybernetically strengthened man
or The Man With No Name
in any case as long as I remember
or as long as I have powered up the machine

the human being is a social animal, as all the theories
like to explain: pecking order, alpha males,
patriarchate, king Arthur but certainly never Arthuress
I open my door
wearing just the long johns and I am fully dressed

I walked today and looked at snow and the various trees
of which I was going to orate in my diary n:o 362
I realised dimly that I was alive, walking, observing
I even smelled, exhaust gases, and heard sounds,
passed by the low, white and grey boxes
commonly called as houses.

I felt ridiculous
I didn't feel like a carrier of The Torch
of Enlightenment, I just watched, a little crapulently
at the snow and felt the cold
then I looked at people who walked on the square
carrying around their consciousnesses

simultaneously in the hell
the painter stared
at the three chubby markers, coloured neon blue
neon green and Christmas red
Satan gave him a canvas and commanded: Create!

I WAKE AT NIGHT

I wake at night
to a world filled with yelps
of material, which is transforming
to gas faster than the speed of sound
I am wondering how those were placed there
is it some holographic trick or
how it works, clearly I am still thinking
but only in my dream

I am quite lonely, I guess
there are people still living
out there somewhere
my self-esteem has developed downward
I move with a hallucinatory accuracy
but only in worlds that do not exist

if I were a god
I would give everyone a new opportunity
after the common death, the insignificant
but I am not god
and in this gloomy game
there is no trying again.

THEY KEEP SHOUTING

They keep shouting, what
quite ordinary words
leaving their sentences sorely unfinished
when their thoughts escape, abruptly,
and flee to camp fires in deep woods
and they themselves leave for a search,
in the dark, in the flutter of candles
and all I am left with is
well, erm - well, erm

my mind is humming, my ossicles have carbonised
from moanings, from confidings, from half sentences
my head is full of talking mouths

surely also at my last glimmering moment,
when I expected to be
contemplating thoughts, deep and serene
I must shoo some vexing, tacky tune
just like during a spectacularly beautiful summer day
I must flee some damn tough gadfly,
which evades escape until I dive into the cold lake
and press my head under the surface
and still I can hear it,
like through a thin membrane.

AND THE ERA DAWNED

And the era dawned
when mankind invented fire
for drowning the continents to the sea
my friend took me to an inland lake, and along the lake,
through long narrow passages to an island,
a lonely pillar from where we could see all the waters
and the high rocky islets
sharp as teeth, lyrically curved
the land of monstrous birds

the birds sang, the moss and the little trees
with their own, cryptic voices
there were people scattered there and many houses
it was not my familiar little island at all

we entered a monorail, which rushed
over shining, foggy rivers and swampy valleys,
enjoyed it like a circus, like we had come
into the torture of amusement park fun machines

eventually, we arrived to the islet
there was a cottage and in the cottage there was a party,
people drunk, chatted, and laughed and sometimes
a flaming, chunky rocket was fired
sky high and everybody watched, very long
as it fell to the shore and exploded to a pond of fire
all were happy and clapped their hands

as the water rose again, a little higher, and put out the flames

upstairs were the toilets
and when I climbed to the second floor hall
I saw the money on the floor
and their owner, a feeble, timid man
and those weather-beaten, malicious goons
who played catch with the poor fellow

I decided to leave: they already had a bad eye on me
they touched, snatched me, just a little, threatened
but I am penniless, what do you want from me?
just out of spite
I withdrew downstairs
the hands reached for me
to hit, to strike, to grasp

I did not tell anyone
just like no one else who had visited there, either
with this shared secret, known to all of us
the party rumbled on until everyone fell asleep
I slept too, to be awakened
to horrified cries: "Go away! - someone's here!"
I looked around
to realize they shouted about me
it was my face
my nose was gone, only a hole left,
a strange mouth with pointy teeth, skin grey
naked and face alien, dangerous

as the first misunderstood one
of species of the future
I wrapped myself to a miserable white bed sheet
and fled

outside, they set fire
to a new deep red, flaming missile,
let it go and it escaped, bursting
to churning flames right next to the sea water

water rose to extinguish, as it always will
waves already reached the base of the verandah
and the celebrants were happy, they applauded and howled
for this was pure,
this was the last feast
this was made to last

the invitation is for everyone
not a request, but a command
and I will comply.

The Art of Deathmatch

I

I did not know
that after a wake up! shout, one can fall
asleep in 30 seconds but apparently, I was wrong

I shoot 400 imaginary magrams in imaginary Desolace
to swap faction, I am chasing the honorific Loremaster
tell me not: The Light of the East, Man of the year,
Master, Doctor, it's all the same.

I hear music again
my feet are not touching the ground
people down far below are passing by
as a jukebox the size of a galaxy plays tunes

the light
in the hall is falsely
the darkening day has stained the walls
I know all the places where I could go
but I am staying here.

I know
the biggest particle accelerator of our fabulous planet
will be booted this month,
and still at the hot-dog stand, or anywhere
in the known world, down there, on the street
nothing has changed in thousand years

the sounds, the crumpled
paper I just tossed to the kitchen sink

the growls of love from those outside
exiting the bar might blurt, and do

I have beer
I have all the entertainment of the big industry right here
and I am far (just like Gary Larson)

the window is open, I am untied
the space is free, empty and lawless.

II

When I got my latest graphics card
I ruminated its 800 million beats per second,
eight hundred incomprehensible million pulsations more
than the heart
of me who will not digress to the jogging paths
every evening to experience the squabble of nylon
or to listen to the moon above the ponds.

And I uttered the druids' highest words
and set the holy relic on its legitimate seat and prayed
but it did not answer

my 220 silver sun carriage!
It showed me only what I already had seen! Just the same!
And somewhere, AMD semiconductor technician
wakes up every morning laughing, laughing.

After two hours sleep
at six in the morning
even the gamblers are sleeping
or at their morning work, on the way to school,
to university, to their careers

I have no work
I read when I read, I play
I am not intending to go anywhere

I turn the music up
the machinery hums, my head,
the traffic outside

in the window box I see
there are brown, dead pine tree branches
a verdant plastic garland,
a nettle.

III

In deathmatch you get respawns
but in life, we get only one chance as novices,
against an incomparable opponent.

I look at my disk collection
in that tournament, I made 170 thousand frags
before connecting to the global village (no kidding!).

With that TBS I got through one full winter.

What will I do, when I have wasted all my ammo?
When rockets pummel my toes,
and I am too tired to dodge any longer,
just satisfied to explode phlegmatically around?

When I have taught my son everything I know
how much to lead, how to listen footsteps, how to
handle the shock rifle and collect the useful power-ups?

Maybe I will ride on a rocking chair
        while the flak balls fragment around me?
Or shall I take a placid space combat sim
and break free from the battlefield to soar,

to admire the pixel clear stardust sky
everywhere above and around me?

IV

I put my boots on, print the poems written by my friend
and go to the shop to search for margarine

the miserable stores
with their expectations

who decided that I must wander
the space rigged between the fridge,
the shop, an the crap hole, the rest of my days?
I eat a sandwich in the toilet and think
about the characteristics of life

Then I turn on my little mobile telly
there's hustle on the little square, I hear
what they say, announcements, maydays,
from the frontiers at the dark, from outer countries
from the Moon, from another reality
the civilians' shouts, talking heads, scrap metal mountains

the light speeds through my crystal head, unadhered
I turn off the device
I watch my room like a reality
I take my keyboard and play

then I will rest
horizontally

I smoke cigarettes
or I do not, I think
or perhaps not.

V

This night at 02:34 o'clock
I have played through my game
but I move still,
more than 200 km per hour

the room lies quiet and stiff, at the base
of the bed the books

my diesel rushes through the window to the darkness
over the conked out houses and depressed gardens
over all the restaurants

I do not think of winning
I do not think of the past
I do not think of honour
I am not afraid of death
I have no father nor mother
I do not think with reason
I am all heart and deadly intuition
I am addressless, torn
      hail, poet!
      (cheers & laughter)

VI

One of these days when the birds fly upside down
it rains snots and neon, so says the TV
but the passersby are all peaceful

at my ex's home, I moved around cupboards
and cut up shrooms, now I am walking,
a sleeping bag in my bag and two beautiful onions

it is autumn
5 wonderful, warm degrees away from freezing
the trees are slowly sprinkling the summer away
I do not comprehend them but all this they grant me

the crow says something
I do not grasp the language, I return to my room

I play myself to Calypso to hunt but there is night
and pitch dark, I play away to Void,'s apocalyptic nightmare,
to the grim phase between death and life
save souls with colours
I visit a small country, eaten by civil war, I am careless
and ignite a terrain fire, I have to flee next to a zebra herd
they outpace me and rumble toward the savannah
the sun of Africa radiating
through the dust hovering in the air.

Am I still here?

VII

I wake,
do not dare to drink coffee
I go check my account
nothing.
so no fetching the Christmas parcel from the post office
I get my ass kicked in Quake
take my kid to day care, return
get my ass kicked in Quake some more
check the account again
nothing.
get my ass kicked in Quake
pick up the laddie from the nursery
loan a video from the library and send him
to his pal's home to watch it
get my ass kicked in Quake, the return of the son of
fetch the laddie and take us to his home
boil macaroni and create a bizarre sauce
he watches children programmes and begins
to complain he has nothing to do
I do not help, I have no ideas
I watch whatevercomesout
from the television
and read simultaneously the biography of Badding
kid paints, messes up, I rise to clean
I command him to make his sandwich himself

I watch the telly and read
he is listening to the smurfs
finally, I send him to sleep and go tuck him in
bring water
now sleep already, hush
I watch at the tragic story of Lindbergh's child
and trial, death to the murderer
ex comes loaded, we chat, she goes to sleep
I can't sleep, the sofa is uncomfortable
the blanket too small and the cats keep running over me
I finish the biography
I sleep, wake, sleep, wake
about twenty times
I wake, we leave for the morning porridge, to the church
social work centre
it is free
still no money
I have not washed myself for five days
or changed my clothes in a week
not washed clothes this month, I think
the dentist also
seems to sense that
or maybe he has a bad day
I fetch my last 12 dimes from the bank
I buy cigarettes I have waited for since the last night,
milk, coffee, filters, and matches
and ride the bicycle into my home, if I can call it so,
three miles and I'm freezing, it's below zero

I can't close the coat properly
cap is ticklish
I come home, make coffee
the toilet leaks, I close the door,
get my ass kicked in Quake.

www.ingramcontent.com/pod-product-compliance
Lightning Source LLC
Chambersburg PA
CBHW030305030426
42337CB00012B/592